# TUMBLEWEEDS;

## A Therapist's Guide
## To Treatment Of
## ACOAs

by

## Paul J. Curtin, MA, CAC

**QUOTIDIAN**
**STROUDSBURG, PENNSYLVANIA**

**FIRST EDITION**
**ISBN  0-934391-03-3**

National Distributor:
THOMAS W. PERRIN, INC.
P.O. Box 190
Rutherford, NJ  07070
(201) 460-7912 in New Jersey
1 (800) 321-7912 from outside New Jersey

QUOTIDIAN
CHERRY VALLEY ROAD, RD #1
STROUDSBURG, PA   18360

Manufactured by Apollo Books, 107 Lafayette St., Winona, MN  55987

PRINTED IN THE UNITED STATES OF AMERICA

# Tumbleweeds

Blowing through the desert
Driving the emptiness of wind
The solitary flight continues.

Prickly burrs and fasteners of fate,
Clutching reprieves of surface joinings,
Encountering again the emptiness within.

With frenzied circles swirling dancing parched and
      sodden floors,
With wedged capture lurking between the weight
      of rocks,
Live desperate strivings and yearnings to be free.

**Paul J. Curtin**
1985

This book is dedicated to these special people for their special gifts:

For their assistance and patience with this book:
>**Karen Curtin**         **Wendy Ramsey**
>**Cordis Burns**         **Marcia Carlton**

For their support and encouragement:
>**The NYS Coalition for the Children of Alcoholic Families**

For the gift of myself:
>**James** and **Lauretta Curtin,** and **Paul Curtin, SJ.**

For the gift of themselves:
>The hundreds of **ACOA**s who have made our lives at Alcohol Services richer.

# Contents

*"I tried to prevent the crisis by coming here but all it did was make the crisis come sooner."*

# I. INTRODUCTION

## What's Going on Here?

### Prevalence of Definitions

"All dressed up and no place to go." This saying describes the plight of adult children of alcoholics (ACOAs) who have been given a wealth of information about their condition, yet relatively little information about what kind of treatment is necessary. An overwhelming majority of the literature, conferences, and workshops is devoted to the following topics:

1. Defining how growing up in an alcoholic family affects children.
2. Defining how, if at all, this affects children as they grow into adulthood.

3. Exploring the question: If a specific syndrome exists for ACOAs,
   A. do all ACOAs "have it?"
   B. what does it consist of?
   C. is it unique to ACOAs?
   D. how does it compare to other family dysfunctions or emotional disorders?
4. Determining whether treatment should be provided from an alcoholism or family therapy perspective, a combination of the two, or a new perspective, which is currently evolving.

This book will be more a treatment guide than a description of ACOAs. In this sense it will represent a new generation of literature. It grants the existence of an ACOA syndrome and focuses on *what to do about it.*

Why is this so important? As a result of the efforts of early pioneers, many of whom can be found on the boards of directors of the National Association for Children of Alcoholics[1] and the New York State Coalition for the Children of Alcoholic Families[2], a movement has been created for children of alcoholics. This movement can be characterized by its tenacity, rapid growth, and thirst for information. Its primary characteristic is that it's composed of ACOAs in overwhelming numbers compared to non-ACOAs. A combination of this thirst for knowledge, the skill of lecturers and authors, and the zeal of conference organizers has resulted in the movement's outgrowing the literature.

Currently we have many ACOAs who can describe their condition yet have little idea what to do about it. Often they have knowledge instead of healing. *They go to conferences instead of therapy!* They understand their emotions instead of experiencing them. They are able to expound upon Claudia Black's rules[3], Janet Woititz's characteristics[4], and Sharon Wegscheider's roles[5]. In fact, conversations at COA conferences often resemble the clichés of singles bars.

"Hi, what sign are you?"

"I'm a Gemini. What about you?"

"I'm a Cancer."

2

This exchange has turned into:

"Hi, what role are you?"

"I'm a hero. What about you?"

"I'm a hero, but there's a bit of mascot in me as well."

ACOAs have been "mistreated, misdiagnosed, or ignored"[6] for years. The fundamental premise of this book is that ACOAs are entitled to therapy that meets their specific needs. They should not have to compose a patchwork quilt of reading, conferences, hopeful conversations, and self-prescribing in an attempt to get the help they need. The movement I referred to earlier is creating a demand for ACOA therapy that must be addressed.

## For all Types of Clinicians

This book is not intended solely for those who work in alcoholism facilities. ACOAs seek help from a variety of different sources. They can be found as patients or clients of psychiatrists, psychologists, mental health workers, and other professionals who work outside the alcoholism field. These clinicians must realize and understand the unique assets, liabilities, and needs of ACOAs.

All patients who enter therapy of any kind should be screened to determine parental alcoholism. (This is in addition to screening for alcoholism in themselves.) If they are ACOAs, a treatment plan should be developed accordingly. Often patients are not able to identify, or will actively reject, the fact that growing up in an alcoholic family *is a significant factor in their problems*. A clinician who is knowledgeable regarding ACOAs will be able to make efforts to defuse this resistance while providing ACOA-specific therapy at the same time. Though this book uses ACOA group therapy as its treatment of choice, the observations and suggestions made can be applied to many settings.

This book is intended for those who wish to help ACOAs in their search to experience and share themselves. It is for those who wish to act as guides for the ACOA's journey to self-awareness and sharing. It will acquaint you with some of the situations you will face, and guide you through some of the problems you will

3

encounter. Most importantly, it will give you the opportunity to take our experience, knowledge, and insight and filter it through your own particular insight and gifts. You can then take what you find useful and freely discard the rest.

## A Warning and a Proposition

It would not be fair to start this book without a warning. Just as there were many Catholic girls in 1945 who, upon seeing the movie "The Bells of St. Mary's", wanted to join the convent as a way of instantly fulfilling themselves, there will be many ACOAs who, upon reading this, will want to become ACOA therapists in order to heal themselves. Don't do it! *Knowledge and helping others is no substitute for personal recovery and healing.* The helping professions are filled with ACOAs who are helping others while not being able to receive help themselves!

This is not to say that the thirst for knowledge of ACOAs should be stifled. I am merely proposing that it be used in a self-enhancing, rather than a self-defeating, manner. This book will be of value to non-professional ACOAs only if it provides them with validation of their experience, insight into their behavior, and an *incentive* to receive appropriate help.

This book proposes that group therapy is the treatment of choice for most ACOAs. Within the context of ACOA group therapy, members will have the opportunity to experience self-awareness and self-acceptance. The group serves as a laboratory where the members can learn to develop healthy, intimate relationships. The book examines the issues of relationships, emotions, confrontation, control, separation, evaluation and departure. These issues are viewed in the context of their role in an ACOA's recovery through the vehicle of group therapy.

> *"I have lived the loneliness of
> a life without sharing."*

*"I've cried here more than anywhere else in my life, yet I've been happier here than anywhere else."*

# II. GROUP THERAPY

## With a Little Help From My Friends

### Group as Community

"Group therapy" means many things to many people. In terms of ACOA therapy, a group gives members the opportunity to create a community based on trust, honesty, intimacy, and acceptance. This community helps members build relationships with each other, challenges members to reveal themselves and their learned defensive patterns, and gives members the opportunity to experience and share feelings freely and unconditionally. Perhaps most importantly, it gives members a chance to be accepted by others more than they can presently accept themselves. As one of our group members said:

5

*"I really believed that if I read everything, I could understand my life and my problems, and not have to experience or share pain."*

ACOAs have an unrealistic perception of themselves and others. An understanding or knowledge of this misperception is not enough. What is necessary is a forum, workshop, or laboratory where relationships can be developed, maintained, and strengthened in an honest and healthy manner. This is precisely why a group is important. It gives its members *a chance to form an inter-personal community where relationships are formed instead of thought about.* Members can experience their defenses and coping mechanisms, learn how those defenses remove them from others, become aware of the pain of the resulting isolation, and take the risk of a journey toward intimacy.

## Self-defined Goals

When ACOAs do have the opportunity to enter treatment they do so for a variety of reasons. The following is a list of self-defined goals ACOAs have shared when they entered therapy. They tend to fall in the categories of relationships, emotions, and self-acceptance.

### Relationships

*To learn how to act appropriately in life situations*
*To experience belonging*
*To learn what "people pleasing" is and to develop alternative helpful behaviors*
*To learn to trust and have intimate relationships*
*To stop rejecting behaviors*
*To experience a safe environment*
*To have someone "call me" on my self-defeating behaviors*
*To learn to trust, love, give and receive in a balanced, healthy way*

To find out what is reasonable in relationships and in
    myself
To learn to stop controlling others
To know that I am not alone
To have an ability to build relationships

## Emotions

To identify, experience and accept feelings
To learn to feel emotions
To express feelings other than anger
To be able to tell people how I feel about things
To stop using humor to avoid feelings

## Self-Acceptance

To learn how to have fun
To learn to be less judgmental of myself and others
To let my walls down
To understand the relationship between past exper-
    ience and present attitudes
To learn and experience forgiveness
To become less overreactive
To develop self-esteem
To stop thinking 10 times before I speak
To stop intellectualizing

These can be summarized as *an inability to experience,
identify, and express emotions immediately and directly.*
This is combined with *an inability to accept themselves as
people* (as opposed to achievers, performers, nurturers, trouble-
makers, lovers, etc.) which results in their either being trapped
within themselves or outside of themselves. "Trapped within
themselves or outside of themselves" is more than just a catchy
phrase. It is crucial that we examine it further, because it provides the
foundation from which we will explore ACOA therapy.

# Sense of Self

## *Trapped Inside*

Any ACOA who enters into treatment has a yearning to be touched *at depth* by another person. At the same time, he is caught between the fear of allowing it to happen and the hope that it actually *can* happen. This conflict is often outside the person's awareness. It is symptomatic of the gap ACOAs have between their perceptions of themselves and reality.

| Perception | Reality |
|---|---|
| 1. I am in touch with my feelings. | 1. They talk about what they understand would be an appropriate feeling. |
| 2. It doesn't bother me. After all, what can you expect? | 2. As long as there is an explanation, excuse, or reason, understanding can be used instead of experiencing emotions. An emotional investment is never made. |
| 3. I don't have anything to say. | 3. There is a process going on in which each thought or emotion is being suppressed as soon as the person becomes aware of it. |
| 4. You should have realized. | 4. Needs are not expressed directly because it raises the risk of rejection. A complicated system of hints and clues is used. This results in the responsibility for attainment of needs and sharing of self being assigned to *other* people rather than the ACOA. |
| 5. I don't understand. What do you want me to do? | 5. Life consists of a series of roles and masks designed to function on a situational rather than a personal level. |

## Trapped Outside

ACOAs have an external focus. It is outside situations that determine their sense of self. They tend to define themselves in terms of *other* people or what *they* do.

| Perception | Reality |
|---|---|
| 1. I have to take care of others. | 1. Taking care of others is easier because it allows the ACOA to be a provider of nurturance rather than a receiver. As long as one focuses on meeting the needs of others, one's own unmet needs can continue to be ignored. |
| 2. I hate making mistakes and hate even more people knowing it. | 2. Mistakes are transformed into a devaluation of self. In this instance the ACOA perceives perfect performance as the only criterion for acceptance by others. |
| 3. I have very high standards that I continually strive to meet. | 3. There is an old Peggy Lee song "Is That All There Is?" which describes this. Achievement is not a substitute for self-acceptance. For the untreated ACOA each step up the ladder of achievement brings a corresponding step down the ladder of emptiness. |
| 4. I think that he had a good point when he criticized me, and I know I should correct it. | 4. There is an entrapment in the world of intellect and concept. This prevents the pain from any conflict being identified and appropriately acted upon. |

| 5. People always tell me that I am (fill in the blank). Therefore I must be. | 5. The sense of self is defined by others, and identity becomes what the circumstance calls for at the moment. |
| --- | --- |

Upon reflection, it becomes apparent that it is not a question of being trapped *either* inside *or* outside of themselves. Those categories are actually two sides of the same coin. The temptation is to say that ACOAs have no sense of "self." However, it seems as if that position represents a slogan more than an accurate description. It is closer to reality to state that ACOAs, when they enter into treatment, are removed from their true selves by a variety of defenses and coping mechanisms. This removal creates *poverty in the areas of trust, vulnerability, intimacy and feelings*. It results in a life characterized by internal control and isolation. There is one point which must be added: there also exists, though often buried beneath the ACOA's conscious awareness, a thirst to experience and share their true selves.

## Present as Key to the Past

When a prospective client, armed with a couple of ACOA conferences under his belt, hears this orientation toward relationships, the response sometimes is: "What about the past? Remember, I'm a child of pain! I want to deal with the anger of having no one there for me. The late night fights, broken promises, and the parenting of my parents need to be addressed." In a sense, he is correct. "A feeling memory bank" must be established. The emotions of the past must be uncovered, experienced, and put to rest. The past must be viewed with honesty, awareness, and acceptance before one can be truly free to live in the present. These essential goals can best be achieved as a by-product of experiencing and sharing feelings in the present. These emotions will arise as a result of the efforts to establish relationships based on trust, honesty, and immediacy in a group setting.

10

The above statement is made with no intention of slighting the value of Restoration Therapy,[1] which calls for a short term, intense, experience designed to unleash repressed experiences and emotions of the past. The point being made is that *freeing oneself from the past does not necessarily guarantee healthy relationships in the present!* Parental alcoholism during childhood retards the mastery of developmental tasks and the formation of healthy interpersonal skills. The work of Stephanie Brown is especially significant since she examines Erickson's stages of development and relates how alcoholism interferes with each one.[2] These deficits need to be addressed. Another way to say this is that ACOAs need to learn how to have healthy relationships and require a structured setting to practice having them. It is not a question of putting the past to rest and living happily ever after. Putting the past to rest is but one of the tasks to be done in the ACOA's journey to self-acceptance and healthy relationships.

## Exceptions to Group

As usual, any general rule has its exception. Here are four major exceptions to the rule that therapy in a group setting works best for ACOA treatment:

1. **Active alcoholics.**
   ACOA therapy is not appropriate for active alcoholics (or other addicts). Alcoholism is a primary disease which robs people of the ability to be honest with themselves and develop healthy intimate relationships with others. ACOA therapy during active alcoholism not only is ineffective due to the nature of the disease, but it fails to take into account the alcoholic's denial system. It provides the alcoholic with an excuse not to address the drinking and enables the alcoholic to continue the progression of this terminal disease.

2. **Newly recovering alcoholics.**
   With researchers discovering that it requires up to 12 months for the bodies of alcoholics to return to normal after drinking

has stopped[2] and behavioral changes resulting from the post acute withdrawal syndrome[3], it is my belief that recovering alcoholics with less than one year of solid recovery should not enter on-going ACOA group therapy. *Recovery from alcoholism is the primary task of the newly sober alcoholic.* An alcoholic's body and brain need time to heal and stabilize before undertaking the complex tasks called for by ACOA group therapy. This is not to say that ACOA issues should not be raised. It is merely a suggestion to follow the slogan found in AA and Al-Anon: "First Things First".

3. **Those who are lost and nearly paralyzed by fear.**
It would be nice if there were a better title, but a description will have to do. There are some ACOAs who are so truly lost and frightened that they cannot tolerate the emotions and interaction to be found in a group. These people need support, caring, acceptance, and a very gentle guide into reality. This can best be accomplished in individual therapy. The goal is to allow the person to attain the personal foundation necessary to make group a worthwhile experience.

4. **Those who have emotional or neurological disorders that preclude them from interacting in a group environment.**

* * *

We also recommend that an ACOA have an individual session with his group leader at regular intervals, for the purposes of on-going evaluation and working on issues raised in the group that need more intense exploration. The frequency of these sessions is determined on a case by case basis.

The following chapters present issues that must be addressed in on-going therapy. The *goal* is to develop healthy relationships within the group. It will also help for you to view the group *as a laboratory in which members strive for an acceptance of self, freedom from the past and for the present, along with the attainment of trust and intimacy.*

*"It doesn't make any difference what I know because I still have to experience the experience of group."*

*"The things I used to do to kill the pain don't work now that I'm in group."*

*"In the beginning I related to people here the same way I related to everyone else. Now I try to relate to everyone else the way I learned to do it here."*

*"I'm an adult tumbleweed. What's a healthy relationship?"*

# III. RELATIONSHIPS

## The Tumbleweeds

### Primacy of Relationships

An ACOA therapy group gives its members the opportunity and structure to develop healthy, intimate relationships with each other. The development of healthy, intimate relationships based on honesty, sharing emotions, vulnerability and confrontation is a primary goal of ACOA therapy. In theory this sounds good to the prospective client. In reality it often marks the first of the many conflicts to be found during the course of treatment.

### Search for Solutions

It has been our experience that most who approach ACOA therapy want to *fix* something. That something could be a situation, relationship, themselves, or any other problem. The underlying assumption could be described as "Tell me what to do and I'll do it". It is part of the on-going search for the "right" answer.

This approach reflects the combination of self-sufficiency and helplessness found in ACOAs. In attempting to get help, they try to structure their environment in such a manner as to perpetuate the very symptoms which are creating problems for them. Their belief is that if they only knew the *rules,* then the situation would get better!

What happens when the client discovers that there are no solutions? What happens when the client is told that the past will only be addressed as a by-product of present emotions? It generally produces anger and fear. These emotions are rarely expressed directly. They often manifest themselves in silence, compliance, and intellectual questioning (i.e., "I don't understand", or "I don't see why").When the therapist is direct and firm regarding the importance of developing relationships, the clients become aware that they are not in charge of their therapeutic process. (It comes down to a question of control. Control is the key issue for ACOAs and there is a chapter devoted to it later on.) Control is threatened when the clients are made aware that their recovery process is bound to the recovery process of others. Developing relationships shatters the attempt at self-adjustment based on intellectual information.

It is time for another grandiose statement! With few exceptions, *ACOAs are incapable of having healthy, intimate relationships* . This is not a statement of condemnation. Growing up in a family characterized by emotional dishonesty, self-sufficiency, unrealistic expectations, lack of trust, and absence of nurturing and sharing make this inevitable. The cruel twist is that this incapacity to have healthy relationships creates a longing for the ideal intimate relationship. It generally results in relationships with fantasy rather than reality as their base. This longing results in intimate relationships that are romanticized, or relationships that are obviously harmful (or at least unfulfilling) but are desperately maintained.

## Romanticized Relationships

These are the beautiful relationships, ones that are better than better. The people involved always have a new thing that they are working on and they enjoy the pain of working on it. These relationships are generally accompanied by a belief that this particular ACOA is different. "I know that I can't express emotion, be honest about my fears, or trust, but our relationship is great. He brings out the best in me." The most amazing characteristic of these relationships is their lack of problems. When a problem is admitted to, there is a refusal to be specific about it. If they are able to be specific about the problem, they accompany it with understanding rather than emotion.

The fantasy is based on the belief that pain, fear, and anger can't exist in a healthy relationship. There is no conception at depth of what a healthy relationship is. Good is defined as "better than what I am used to". A relationship in which a person gets punched once a day will seem like ecstasy compared to one in which he gets punched ten times a day.

This activity of romanticizing applies not only to relationships, it very often applies to an ACOA's childhood as well. There is a tendency toward emotional numbness and euphoric recall[1] (similar to that of alcoholics) regarding their family. They make the mistake of focusing solely on what happened or the "horror stories". "It wasn't that bad", or "That never happened to me" is heard quite frequently. This allows the ACOA to operate on the basis of technical uniqueness.

The therapist must focus on *what didn't happen.* If anything is universal about ACOAs it's the sense of not having their parents available for them. Alcoholism has robbed the alcoholic parents by stealing their capacity to share themselves and to be present to others. Parents can't give a child what they don't have. It is my belief that an awareness of this parental poverty is hidden inside every ACOA. This accounts for the tenacity with which they hold on to romanticizing. Through group support, sharing, and acceptance an ACOA may be able to embrace the pain of that poverty and become free. Sadly, many times ACOAs are only able to tighten their defenses and reinforce their denial.

*"My parents gave me everything I wanted except themselves."*

It is important to realize that ACOA therapy often creates conflicts between spouses. When the romanticization of a relationship is challenged, quite often the client leaves therapy rather than view the present involvement with a critical eye. If the client remains, the changes caused by therapy and recovery often threaten the balance achieved in the marriage. This will force each person to take a personal inventory.


## Clinging to Bad Relationships

A bad relationship is at least a relationship! Because ACOAs have poor self-concepts and low self-esteem, bad relationships are often held onto out of a sense of desperation or familiarity. This desperation is based on the thought that there may not be another chance at a relationship. Since their sense of self is defined externally, it is essential for them to have someone to hold onto. They intuitively sense that if they stop struggling (moving, working, running, etc.) they will have to come face to face with themselves. The pain of remaining in a bad relationship is less threatening than the pain of facing their past and their isolation from themselves.

The familiarity is based on a lifetime of unhealthy, unfulfilling, or shallow relationships. What criteria do ACOAs have to judge relationships? It is heard many times that they have no idea what to expect. *"I never knew friends were allowed to fight. I thought if we did, it was all over."* Since self-sufficiency runs rampant, there is no conception that a relationship can be depended upon to meet vulnerable personal needs. It is not uncommon to see long periods of numbing despair resulting from an on-going bad relationship. This numbing despair *is preferred* to the relatively brief period of acute pain which would result from an open, honest termination of a relationship.

## Relationships in Group Therapy

When ACOAs enter group therapy, the relationships they are called to form will be different from any others that they may have experienced. These relationships will be based upon the following guidelines:

1. expressing and sharing emotions.
2. interacting with group members honestly.
3. taking risks and becoming vulnerable.
4. avoiding "homogenizing" thoughts and feelings before expressing them.
5. having honest confrontation with each other.

All too often people want to use group as a dumping ground, a place to go to give testimony about their trials and tribulations. The therapist must guard against the group's degenerating into individuals giving *descriptions* of their private world to other individuals. The person's world must become open. A group member must invite others into his world and actively enter the worlds of others

It is easier to share the event of childhood incest than to experience and share the fear of telling a fellow group member (who you are afraid of) that you think he is not being honest. In other words, it is easier to deal with an *event* than a *person*. Sharing what happened is nice, but *sharing who you are is better*. An ACOA therapy group, which degenerates into members talking about their past and present situations, quickly becomes a symphony of self-centeredness. Members operate safely within their defenses, sharing only what they want to get out, but never letting anybody in.

ACOA group therapy is aimed at letting people in. It aims to develop relationships which thrive on honesty, vulnerability, and need. It is not enough for a client to need the group. It is necessary that a client need the relationships that are being developed with other members. When a client says "I don't see a need to share this with the group," the client is reminded that what he really said is: "I don't want to share this with you and you and you." There is no such thing as "the group". In reality, "the group" is actually other human beings who come together once a week in community.

It turns out that recovery is not an individual procedure. Relationships formed in a structured environment are its foundation. The therapy session is a laboratory where a member can learn how to have relationships. It is a place where risks can be taken safely. It is a place where old, self-defeating ways of relating can be pointed out, acknowledged, mourned and discarded. It is a place where healthy ways of interacting can be developed.

## Problems Regarding Group Relationships

At this point it will be useful to look at the problems regarding relationships which develop among group members. These must be addressed within the group setting.

*1.   Family Members:* Family members should not be placed in the same ACOA therapy group. There are often different perceptions and unresolved issues which would hinder the functioning of the group. The unspoken methods of communication and the intuitive common frame of reference produce a universe that is often closed to others. It is better that work with family members be done in a family therapy setting.

*2.   Dating:* It is essential that the therapy group not be used as a dating service. Group members are in the process of learning to develop relationships. If a person is incapable of having healthy intimate relationships, that same person isn't capable of having healthy, intimate, *romantic* relationships! Group members are discouraged from developing romantic relationships with fellow group members.

The desire for a "quick fix" also applies to romantic relationships with people outside of group. There is a belief that a lover will make everything all right. It is a lot easier for the ACOA to deal with the pain of isolation through sex and romance than for that person to become vulnerable to fellow group members. Group members who believe they are alone because they don't have a partner (or perfect spouse) ignore the reality of the relationships that they are attempting to build among fellow group members.

3. *Members' socialization:* Members continuing to pursue relationships with fellow group members socially can be the *best* possible thing. It can also be the *worst*. In the beginning, it is a joy to watch members have parties, go out to dinner, and make phone calls to each other. It is exciting to see them have fun and start to turn to each other for help. They are beginning to form a true community.

A problem arises when they begin not to share things in group. Often they say they do not share things in group because they have already talked about it on the phone to another group member. People won't take a risk during group because they don't want to spoil going out to dinner afterwards. Group members won't confront another member because they know what a hard time that particular member is going through. Action won't be taken because they believe there will be other opportunities during the week, outside of group time, to address what needs to be addressed.

It is important for the therapist to stress that *the primary work of recovery must be done in group* . Members owe each other 90 minutes of sharing during the group session. In the structured environment of therapy, the vulnerability is greater. The members cannot "call the shots". It is harder to get away with old methods of behavior. The risks members encounter talking on the phone are much less than the risks encountered with their peers during group. The therapist must not allow complacency to develop and must also be willing to confront group members. This confrontation is usually based on the therapist's observation that socializing is taking the place of therapy or that therapy is becoming yet another social event.

*"People come through my life not into it."*

*"I hear talk of nurturance and caring, and it produces a feeling in me, but I have no idea what the words mean."*

*"My relationships are like a game of hide and seek—I'll hide and you seek the real me."*

*"Most of the relationships I held onto didn't exist."*

*"The people I want to accept me are the ones I tell the least to."*

*"I use people, then they get tired of it, and then I get mad at them"*

*"I leave group hoping people won't call me, and then I'm hurt when they actually don't."*

*"I've been too busy to feel lately."*

# IV. EMOTIONS

## Too Busy to Feel

### Emotions as Cornerstone

Emotions are the key to healthy intimate relationships. One of the main barriers keeping ACOAs from having healthy relationships is that they are emotionally retarded. This means that in general their emotions are repressed, unidentified, pasteurized, confused, misdirected, and rarely expressed directly. There is a wellspring of emotion from the past which hinders the experiencing and expressing of appropriate emotions in the present. The realm of emotions becomes a shadow world of which the ACOA is vaguely aware but is barred from entering. This results in relationships characterized by intellectualization and shallowness.

ACOA group therapy must be designed to give its members the opportunity to identify and express their emotions directly and appropriately. This is the key to successful recovery. Intimacy cannot be established if emotions are not shared. One of the first actions a therapist must take is to define what can be called an emotion or feeling.

As a general rule, a feeling should be identified in two words or less. ACOAs tend to disguise thoughts as feelings. An example of this is: "I feel that you are ignoring what I am saying." There is no such emotion as "that you are ignoring what I am saying." In reality, if group members are feeling anger or fear because they *think* they are being ignored, it is a lot safer to say to a person, "I feel you are ignoring me," than to say, "I am angry at you because I think that you are ignoring me." If there were a satchel of tools that an ACOA therapist carried, one of the most used would be the phrase, "That is what you *think*. Can you share with us what you are *feeling*?" A group member learns that thoughts are not feelings by stripping away the barrier of the intellect. It brings him face to face with the realm of emotion. The ACOA is now ready to begin the process of identifying and expressing emotions.

## Problems Identifying Emotions

Children of alcoholics spend their childhood in families where broken promises, unfulfilled expectations, denial of reality, physical or emotional abuse or neglect, and emotional turmoil are the norm. It has been said that they develop survival rather than living skills.[1] One survival technique is to put the pain, anger, and hurt in that shadow world in an attempt to get away from them in order to function. In reality, all emotions, not just selected ones, wind up there. As they grow into adulthood, these children of alcoholics find their emotional repertoire extremely limited. (It brings to mind the phrase in the theatre, "She went through her entire range of emotions from A to B.")

This is not to say that the emotions are not present. They are present but unavailable to the ACOA. In ACOA group therapy, the member is given encouragement and support to look into this previously closed world. This process illuminates a number of

24

devices used to block the acknowledgment of emotions. The following are areas of difficulties that ACOAs face in attempting to identify their emotions:

1. On-going fear and anger become normal. They become a condition of existence rather than a problem. They permeate so many things that the best way to identify them is by their absence.

2. A tightly woven fabric of thoughts and explanations, dealing with theories and situations, keeps ACOAs from identifying and experiencing emotions. They tend to express what they are *thinking* about a situation rather than what emotion they are *experiencing*. There is also a tendency to guess at what they are feeling. It becomes an intellectual process of attempting to find the "right" answer, rather than experiencing what is happening inside of them.

3. Group members often say that they don't know what they are feeling. This cannot be taken at face value. It is more correct to say that they cannot put a name on what they are feeling. If that is the case, then it is necessary to go to a description of physical sensations. As one member released his anger during a group session by yelling and pounding a pillow, another member said she didn't know what she was feeling. However, upon probing, the member disclosed sweating, mild nausea, and faintness. It was then pointed out that these symptoms usually accompany fear. It was not a question of not feeling emotions. It was a question of identifying and giving a name to those sensations.

4. Attempts are made consciously to repress emotions in order to "get by." Emotions are viewed as something which cannot be acknowledged because that acknowledgment would result in paralysis. Emotions are viewed as interrupters of life rather than an essential part of life. A good example is the ACOA who received news of possible cancer and "refused"

25

to feel fear and anger until after the exploratory procedure scheduled two weeks in the future.

5. In an attempt not to feel pain or anger, ACOAs deny that they have expectations of people or have emotional needs of their own. They may have expectations of situations (i.e., work, politics, housekeeping) and even express anger regarding these areas, but they are generally silent regarding the areas of emotional sharing, vulnerability and giving. The expectations they have are in regard to *what they do* instead of *who they are*. An ACOA will rant and rave because the spouse did not complete a chore, but will respond to a lack of emotional support with, "It's my problem anyhow. What could they do?"

## Problems Expressing Emotions

This is the most exciting part for the ACOA therapist. In watching clients begin to express emotions, the therapist watches them come alive. When an ACOA expresses emotion, he begins to become real. The intellectualization and rationalization are cast aside. It is a privilege to receive the raw emotion rather than the processed farina. It is a joy to see clients taking risks and being themselves, rather than what they believe they should be!

In a group therapy setting, ACOAs are generally torn. They want to belong but know, at least at some level, that the emotions they have suppressed must be experienced and expressed. The bind that grips ACOAs is their *belief* that if they express emotion then relationships will be threatened, coupled with the *fact* that if they don't, healthy relationships will be impossible. This tension comes from the ACOA's belief that there are *bad* emotions (such as anger, fear, and sorrow) and that to have or express them would shatter a relationship.

The therapist must be aware of the tendency of ACOAs in group to express emotion regarding situations rather than people. This is usually a result of an attempt to express emotion while at the same

26

time minimizing risks. The expression of emotion must be viewed in the context of developing intimate relationships with other group members. It is a lot safer to be mad at "the group" than it is to be mad at specific individuals. It is less risky to be hurt by "people not being there for me" than it is to express hurt to the group member who did not follow through on a promise. Along the same lines, it is safer to be furious at the "loss of a childhood" than to be furious at a mother and father.

A majority of the time in group will be spent attempting to have presently-felt emotions expressed immediately. Expressing emotions in the present will provide the ACOA with a key to unlock the emotions of the past still stored in the shadow world. In the laboratory of group therapy, the client will be forced through loving confrontation to experience the fear of expressing emotion with fellow members. The member will become aware of the defenses used to deny the expression of honest emotion. The following are some areas of difficulty ACOAs face in attempting to express emotion:

1. ACOAs generally wait for an explosion to express emotion. That is to say, expression of emotion is usually a result of an accumulation of emotions that can no longer be held in. In their eyes, an emotion is an emotion only in the extreme. The emotions that eventually force their way to expression are usually ones of great power (i.e., rage, sorrow, exhilaration). However, during their fight to the surface, they must work their way through such an elaborate system of defenses, roadblocks, and checks and balances that they are greatly defused. It is important to remember that these emotions are not the only ones there. They are simply the only ones that have been able to escape!

The therapist's task is not to teach ACOAs how to feel. The task of the therapist is to make them aware of what they are feeling and to be able to express it. The task is fairly tedious because it involves interrupting defense systems that are more sophisticated and quicker reacting than the proposed

Strategic Defense Initiative (Star Wars) or an ABM system. Quite simply, it is to identify hurt when it happens before it simmers in the cauldron and turns into sorrow; it is to identify anger at its first instance before it boils into rage; it is to experience happiness when it is felt and before it is dismissed because it is not ecstasy.

In encouraging ACOAs to express emotions immediately, the therapist and group members issue an invitation to leave the private shadow world. It is a world where emotions are *thought* away. It is an invitation to share the true self rather than a finished product which is based on others' expectations. In issuing that invitation, group members are asking to participate in the person's life *as it happens*.

2.  Upon the ACOA hearing this invitation to share the "day to day" emotions, he asks instantly, "Why bother?" The underlying questions are, "What good will it do?" "How will it change things?" and "How will that affect the actions of others?" An ACOA operates with the premise that emotions are expressed to get desired results. The expression of emotion is in the realm of situations rather than people. The therapist must address this issue.

The expression of appropriate emotion in an alcoholic family is generally not rewarded. The expression of emotion on the part of a child often results in punishment, isolation, and fear. At an early age the child learns that expressing honest emotion doesn't pay off. It is not surprising that when the child grows up and is lucky enough to be in an ACOA therapy group, the invitation to express emotions is immediately viewed with fear and skepticism. In order to escape from pain, an elaborate rationalization system is established. ACOAs claim to have no anger toward their parents because, "How can you be mad at someone who has a disease?" They claim to have no sorrow about an ungiving spouse because "I never expected sharing from him". They believe they have no emotions because, "What difference does it make? It's not worth it." The therapist can rest assured that the emotions are there. In fact, when the area of pain and sorrow regarding loved ones is approached, it creates a crisis for the client. This is a turning point; quite often the ACOA leaves therapy.

The purpose of expressing emotions as they occur is not to change a situation. The primary purpose is to develop a manner of living which is designed to increase intimacy. Each time clients say, "I'm happy I'm here," "I'm mad that you are silent," or "I'm hurt that you said that," they are taking a risk. They are becoming vulnerable. It is allowing others to see who they are. This is the essence of intimacy. The underlying principle of this step is that ACOAs have self-worth. They are valuable as people. They have a right to share who they are. In expressing these emotions, they are allowing others into the process of their lives instead of presenting them with the finished product. They are forming relationships.

3. There is a belief among ACOAs that directly expressing anger, hurt or sadness about another person will harm that individual. This belief cannot be accepted at face value. This line of reasoning must be explored:

If I express my anger, I will hurt this person.
If I hurt this person, he will be angry at me.
If he is angry at me, he will reject me.
If he rejects me, I will be alone.
I don't want to be alone.

---

**Therefore, I will keep my anger to myself.**

Emotions are viewed as dangerous. They become divided into *good* and *bad*. Anger, pain, fear, and sorrow are considered bad, while happiness, excitement, and joy are considered good. ACOAs come into group after a lifetime of presenting selected emotions. In a very real way, the emotions ACOAs do express are manipulative. They are designed to affect a given situation or change someone else's behavior. When one group member is confronted by another, the response often starts with, "I'm happy you were able to say that." This usually isn't true. Admitting to being furious would be closer to the truth. Since expression of anger would only make the situation worse in their eyes, the response is conciliatory and designed to make the encounter pass with minimal friction.

Fear of rejection is the emotion behind this misguided attempt to spare the feelings of others; the principle is: "I don't matter." It doesn't matter what they feel, because their goal is to avoid the conflicts they perceive will result in rejection.

*"If I show who I really am, no one will like me."*

Their needs are unimportant or denied. Instead of working to bring people closer to them, they are struggling to keep people from leaving!

It is the job of the therapist to create a group atmosphere where the client can learn that expressing emotions may hurt people, but it won't drive them away. In healthy relationships the expression of emotions will bring people closer. Hurt and reconciliation are part of the group therapy process. As recovery progresses, they learn that *not* expressing emotions harms others. It deprives other group members of *the real person inside*. They discover that the very tools developed not to lose people are responsible for keeping them away!

4. ACOAs generally operate under the assumption that before an emotion can be expressed, it must be correct. That means that a series of conditions must be met before an emotion can be expressed or viewed as valid. There can now be added to the previous categories of good and bad emotions the categories of right and wrong emotions. "I have no right to feel this way," "I shouldn't feel this way," "I feel bad feeling this," and, "How could I feel this?" are all reflective of that assumption.

When group members are confronted about a defensive shield they are using, they often acknowledge that they are using it and agree to change it. *Their agreement displaces emotion.* Since the confrontation was "correct," they do not acknowledge their anger at being confronted. There is an attempt to "agree" all emotion out of the situation. A discussion about the validity of the person's comment is irrelevant. Bringing out *what the person was feeling when confronted* and how he reacted *at that moment* is vital.

A story is the best way to make this point: The therapist was fifteen minutes late for the start of an ACOA group. The clients were waiting in the hall and starting to feel angry. Upon arrival, the therapist opened the door and everyone took his seat. After a period of silence, which seemed like an eternity, one group member mustered the courage to express anger at the therapist for being late.

The others drew courage from the first one and expressed their anger also. Some were even able to express anger they had bottled up for some time regarding past experiences of being forgotten either by parents or loved ones. The anger was real and very direct.

After it subsided, the therapist explained about the car accident that caused the delay and expressed regret at not being able to be on time for group. There was another seemingly eternal silence. All at once the group members started to apologize for being mad and tried to take back the anger they had expressed. The therapist interrupted and said, "You have given me a great gift by being mad at me and expressing it. The accident does not invalidate your emotions. By sharing your anger directly, you have taken a risk and shared yourself. It has brought us closer together. In sharing your emotions when you felt them and not after analyzing them, you shared *who you are* and not who you think you *should be*."

5. The goal of ACOA group therapy is not to talk about emotions. The goal is to experience and share them. This is difficult because it involves a struggle against the tendency to intellectualize. It is more productive to feel and experience joy than to embark on a quest to understand why joy is felt.

It is not unusual to see very painful events (incest, violence, divorce) disclosed with a very flat affect. It is not unusual to hear group members say that they are sad or afraid and look as if they are discussing the weather. Often group members say they are angry and have a smile on their faces. The reverse of this is also true: they often vehemently deny they are mad while at the same time their voices are raised, faces are red, teeth are clenched, feet are tapping, and fists are clenched!

The group therapy setting is particularly useful in this area. Other group members can hold a mirror for the client to see his behavior. It can be pointed out that the person claims to be mad, yet is still smiling. Members begin to demand that others share what they are feeling instead of what they think about what they are feeling.

Expressing emotion is a risk, yet it is also a key to freedom. There are many ACOAs who read the literature and are quick to say, "My parents abandoned me a long time ago, but they never left home." However, they have never mourned that loss! In group, members are urged to interrupt a person when they believe that person is telling a story and not sharing emotions. Sharing intimate details of a life story can be good, but it often serves as a distraction from the pain presently felt. Expressing the pain and hurt ACOAs feel about their lives can give them freedom to move on. Merely telling stories about their lives usually results in staying stuck.

## Emotions and Recovery

Identifying and expressing emotions is of paramount importance in ACOA group therapy. The success of an ACOA's recovery revolves around these issues. The therapist will encounter the most varied and sophisticated types of resistance when the realm of emotions is approached. Here also the richest rewards are found, because when emotions are unlocked, the client becomes free and begins to blossom. It is truly liberating to see ACOA group members discover—at the end of a session filled with rage, conflict, and sorrow directed toward each other—that no one died from the emotion. Reconciliation is happening, and they are closer to each other than they ever were.

*"I identified having feelings as hurting and being out of control."*

*"Living in denial helps me get through a lot of things."*

*"When I was growing up, what I did was all that mattered. What I felt didn't count at all."*

*"I have episodes of feelings which hit at odd moments."*

*"I'd rather deal with fear than with anger."*

*"When you talked about the pain you are in, you sounded like you were saying 'Pass the potatoes...'"*

*"I don't know if it's anything major, but I need to share how sad I feel."*

*"I'm scared to come to group because I get confronted on defenses that are very dear to me."*

# V. CONFRONTATION

## This Means War!

### Confrontation and ACOAs

Confrontation is misunderstood. When an ACOA hears the word it is accompanied by visions of yelling, screaming, and devastation. Confrontation has a bad reputation. It is generally viewed as something extra-ordinary to be used only as a last resort. ACOA group therapy uses confrontation quite extensively. In fact, confrontation *must* be incorporated into all healthy intimate relationships.

For our purposes, confrontation is defined as honestly telling people what you *think* about their behavior and how you *feel* about it. In ACOA group therapy both elements must be present. It is not enough merely to share perceptions regarding a person's behavior. The emotions that behavior generates must be shared as well. This is what separates confrontation from criticism. It is what makes it an attempt to reach out rather than an effort to push away.

Why is it so difficult for ACOAs? The answer is to be found in the families in which they were raised. An alcoholic family operates in such a manner as to prevent honest confrontation. The drinking is the most important issue in the family and yet is rarely addressed. Bizarre or inappropriate behavior is either ignored or explained away. It is as if all the family members are partners in a conspiracy of silence. Children learn very fast that there are areas outside the realm of discussion or questioning. They learn that it is easier not to express disappointment, anger, confusion, or disagreement about their parents' or others' behavior. They keep their perceptions, thoughts, and feelings to themselves. Even worse, they begin to deny them and start to doubt themselves. The needs, perceptions, and feelings of others take precedence over their own.

## Benefits to the Confronting Individual

Confrontation helps an individual in a number of different ways:

1. When ACOAs confront another person it is an act of self-affirmation. It is affirming the fact that ACOAs have needs, that they can be affected by the behavior of others, and that they have a right to speak out on their own behalf. *Confrontation is an act of self-worth*. It allows the individual to set limits and express needs. This is an enormous step for ACOAs. It gives them an opportunity to shape relationships instead of "falling into" them. They no longer have to be content to accept whatever they are given in a relationship. They can pursue their own needs and desires, as well as enter into relationships as equals.

2. Confrontation allows ACOAs to test their perception of reality. "I assume that you thought...," "I figured you were...," and, "You probably didn't mean to...," are all very dangerous in healthy relationships. ACOAs come from a

lifetime of hidden meanings, mixed messages, hints, guesses, innuendos, and unspoken communication. There is a great fear of being direct. It is scary to have a person be mad at you, but it is even more frightening to have that anger expressed directly!

Confrontation in this area is difficult. In the last chapter we discussed the tendency to view emotions as right or wrong. "I am mad because I think you are ignoring me," is difficult to say because it is sharing with another person. A risk is being taken in order to validate that perception. The answer could be "yes," in which case it gives the two people something to explore, or "no," in which case it gives the person an opportunity to let go of the anger. In either situation it ensures that the relationship is grounded in reality instead of misperception.

3. Confrontation gives ACOAs an opportunity to face issues rather than ignore them. They tend to prefer the dull chronic pain of an ignored, on-going problem than to face the short term pain of addressing and resolving it. Ignored problems suffocate healthy relationships. Intimacy is traded away for surface calmness. They prefer the *appearance* of a relationship instead of the *experience* of a true relationship.

When confrontation does not take place and issues are not addressed, chronic anger and hurt result. The anger and hurt are generally wrapped in numbness and covered with denial. People ignore or deny their own expectations, needs and desires in order not to face the pain of a situation. This sinking into numbness is usually done in silence, leaving few traces of the hope that once was present.

Confrontation breaks the conspiracy of silence. It says that *if a relationship cannot tolerate honesty and openness, it is not worth having.* It is a recognition that *the pain of addressing a problem is more valuable than the results of ignoring it.*

In ACOA group therapy members are usually hesitant to confront each other. A humorous analogy would be that of a huge moose— which everyone is ignoring— standing in the middle of the room. A therapist must often ask if anyone smells the moose. The moose is generally a major issue which members are going to great lengths to avoid. Some examples are: a pattern of absence or tardiness, a member's on-going intellectualization, a member's continuing silence, a budding romance in the therapy group, or a member's playing therapist. Everyone is aware of the moose and no one addresses it. The confrontation is avoided because no one wants to rock the boat or risk a member's wrath. *Confrontation will occur when a member realizes that relationships based on honesty and addressing issues are more important to him than surface relationships based on fear.*

4. Confrontation enables ACOAs to step out of themselves and enter into relationships with others. *It is a decision to share who they are* with other people. It is sharing all of their thoughts and emotions instead of only the "correct" ones. Confrontations call for interaction in depth. Very few people enjoy confronting and being confronted. It often involves pain, anger and fear, yet it paves the way for caring, love and joy. It is a sign that people care enough for themselves and others to risk displeasure and anger in order to achieve a relationship based on honesty.

ACOA group therapy is an excellent vehicle for confrontation. It is a laboratory where its members can learn to share and interact with each other. Through their presence in group and by their actual words, members invite each other to confront them. This is not to say that they won't get angry or be resistant. It is, however, a commitment to remain in relationship and resolve the problems. Confrontation involves risk. The sharing necessary for healthy confrontation requires vulnerability. The group provides nourishment for that vulnerability by providing an atmosphere of caring and support which allows members to draw closer to each other and leave their own isolation.

## Benefits of Being Confronted

Confrontation benefits more than just the individual who is doing the confronting. Being confronted is essential to an ACOA's recovery. Being confronted is to be presented with a gift (granted, it is one people would often gladly do without). The gift is of value on a number of different levels.

1. _Being confronted_ gives ACOAs an opportunity to become aware of their defenses and see how their behavior affects others. By entering into a relationship with others, they are requesting to be shown what they can't see in themselves. Confrontation encourages individuals to be real and makes it difficult to deny what they are feeling.

   Confrontation provides people with insight into their emotions and behaviors. When it is pointed out that a member is telling a story about a painful situation instead of sharing the pain, the confrontation is an invitation to be real. Through confrontation members are made aware that their efforts to show concern (by lecturing, questioning, giving advice) are actually keeping others away from them. Members are frequently unaware of their defenses—defiance when confronted, nonstop talking when afraid, or changing subjects when in pain. Confrontation provides a mirror through which this behavior can be recognized and then changed.

Through confrontation, members become aware that their actions affect people. Their silence makes people discount them; their seething rage makes people afraid of them; their flip or sarcastic remarks make people mad; their self-sufficiency hurts people; their use of humor shields them from people. Most of these defenses came into existence in an attempt to keep at least some kind of relationship going. Confrontation shows that in reality these defenses prevent healthy relationships from forming.

The overwhelming majority of confrontation in ACOA group therapy is in response to a member's not being real. ACOAs are often confronted on the following common maneuvers:

—changing the subject when uncomfortable
—asking questions in an attempt to understand rather than feel
—using sarcasm instead of expressing anger
—explaining away emotion
—rescuing someone from the group's attention
—laughing when confronted or feeling pain
—analyzing their life from the perspective of a disinterested party
—vehemently defending a position or concept while not looking at themselves or their emotions
—refusing to ask for, or allowing others to, help
—presenting the group with a "finished package" instead of allowing others into the process of their life
—telling a story about great pain, anger or joy in their lives with a deadpan expression

In all probability, without confrontation these behaviors will never be addressed, and change will never be considered.

2. *Being confronted* frees ACOAs from the belief that being perfect is a prerequisite for acceptance. They generally consider it horrible to make a mistake but even more horrible to have other people be aware of it. Confrontation recognizes

the fact that hurt and forgiveness, as well as anger and reconciliation, must be present in all healthy, intimate relationships.

ACOA group therapy provides the members with first-hand experience that confrontation is not the end of the relationship. A member can actually observe confrontation and participate in its bringing people closer together. A member's confrontation does not mean expulsion from the group. It does not mean that the person doing the confronting will never speak to him again. It shows that anger can be addressed in a healthy manner. Instead of going beneath the surface and seething, it can be released.

Confrontation dispels the myth that healthy, intimate relationships must be free of open conflict. Healthy confrontation requires that both parties become vulnerable. It is this vulnerability and openness that draw people together. As this process grows, ACOAs discover that it is not strength that builds healthy relationships; it is vulnerability. When people are removed from the bondage of perfection, they are free to grow and explore.

3.  *When a person* is not *confronted* in ACOA group therapy, that person is actually being harmed. To refuse to confront a person in order not to cause hurt feelings results in more harm than the pain of any possible confrontation. When a person does not confront a group member, *that person is being dishonest*. Honesty is not merely being truthful in what is said. It also involves saying what is seen in others. The statement, "I didn't want to hurt your feelings", is usually not true in the context of group. "I'm afraid of your reaction", "I'm tired of trying to reach you", or "I don't have the interest" are usually closer to the truth. It is important to emphasize that there is nothing wrong with those three statements. It is only wrong when they are not expressed!

41

Silence is damaging. It is a refusal to let people know where they stand. In a very real way they are being *written off*. ACOAs are very skilled at dealing with painful or uncomfortable situations by adapting. They adapt and remain inside of themselves. It is not unusual to see group members react to a person's incessant talking or inappropriate interrupting by silence or withdrawal. Not confronting this member results in group members forfeiting the session. It also allows that member to remain ignorant of behavior which drives people away.

We have talked about expectations, but members of ACOA therapy groups also have an obligation to each other. It is not an obligation in the area of performance. It is an obligation to share who they are and what they see in others. In not doing that they deny their fellow members an opportunity to grow and learn. Confrontation based on a misperception may hurt people or make them angry, but silence harms and damages them.

4. *When ACOAs are confronted*, they are also receiving the gift of commitment from the other person. The person is actively indicating that the member is worthy of notice, that the member matters, and that the member has an effect on his life. Confrontation involves people taking a risk by sharing themselves. *It is an affirmation of a relationship* . The confronter cares enough about the person to risk that member's wrath. It is so easy to ignore something or not share the pain another person's actions have caused. After all, it will probably be forgotten by the next week's session.

The "easy" way is not taken because there is a commitment to honesty and intimacy. There is a willingness to face pain in order to achieve growth. Confrontation shows a willingness to work together; people become partners in a relationship. The relationship becomes a living entity which

42

can be molded, shaped and developed. Confrontation becomes something which the members use to bring them together instead of ignoring it in order to keep each other from leaving.

The call to confrontation issued in ACOA group therapy is a challenging one. Through it members can experience the fear they have about being direct with another person. They are challenged to give up the hints, assumptions and silences that characterize their relationships. It is a time for celebration when a member can say, "It makes me afraid to say this to you but....". The recognition involved in sharing that fear is *a victory in and of itself!* Confrontation often results in self-awareness rather than effect on others. It is primarily for personal growth instead of an attempt to change the behavior of others.

Confrontation shares with others who you are. It means that the ACOA will give up the game of I'll Hide And You Go Seek. It is an invitation to relationship rather than a plea for one. Confrontation allows the ACOA therapy group to grow from the Symphony of Self-Centeredness composed of individual stories to a Family of Caring People whose relationships are based on honesty, sharing and interaction.

*"I refuse to admit when I'm angry."*

*"I don't want to make waves so I don't say anything."*

*"When someone says, 'I need to talk to you' I get terrified."*

*"I'm tired of all of you dumping on me."*

*"It is strange to think of confrontation as an expression of love rather than an attack."*

*"In the midst of incredibly long bouts of talking, I've managed to totally hide myself."*

# VI.  CONTROL

## The Lonely Controller

### Control and ACOAs

Control permeates all areas of ACOA group therapy.[1] It is difficult to isolate because it is a part of so many problems. Perhaps the best way to begin is to clarify the concept. In this context, the word "control" indicates ACOAs' attempts to structure themselves, their relationships and their environment in such a manner as to reduce the necessity for healthy dependence and vulnerability. The emotion which provides the main source of fuel for on-going control is *terror*. This terror is based upon issues of abandonment/rejection as well as problems regarding self-worth and self-acceptance.

The rigid control shown by ACOAs is a result of defenses developed in response to growing up in an alcoholic family. The lack of consistency, trust, and caring, as well as the chaos and unpredictability found in alcoholic families, leaves a child with few choices. Control is necessary for protection and survival. However, *what was once used as a necessity in childhood becomes a liability in adulthood.*

*Control is used to avoid vulnerability.* It prohibits ACOAs from giving themselves to other people in an intimate, healthy manner. It results in a life based on calculation and protection rather than spontaneity and openness. The saddest thing about control is how hard people work to maintain it! The toil is not based upon achieving anything positive. It is a lonely struggle *to prevent an imagined catastrophe from occurring.* Three of the imagined catastrophes are: fear of rejection, loss of self, and the overwhelming of the individual.

## Catastrophes

1. *Rejection.* Acceptance and love become commodities which must be purchased by a person's performance. If it is true that love is a gift freely given, and if it is also true that acceptance is in the realm of who people are rather than what they achieve, then the attempt to purchase them through performance is doomed.

   ACOAs come from an environment where alcoholism robs the parents of their ability to express love through sharing of themselves. Attention, gifts, favors, and recognition of accomplishments become the medium for care to be shown. A sense of self develops from what can *be done*. There is no true sense of self. Identity is based on achievement. In fact, there is a belief that if other people knew truly who the ACOA was, they would leave him. Their relationships are based on having to earn friendship. Their life becomes an on-going struggle to achieve self worth through external attainments. However, each attainment does not do what it is supposed to do. It only highlights the emptiness of their lives!

" "*If I do not continue to perform, I will be nothing and have nothing,*" is a good way to describe this perspective. Control is essential because there is no room for mistakes. Spontaneity, experimentation, and risks become enemies. Achievement cannot be savored because it is viewed as a momentary reprieve from the impending catastrophe of rejection. Control is used to forestall that rejection. The ACOA strives to say the right thing, avoid conflict, become invaluable, and do for others in an attempt to belong. This leads inevitably to a life of reaction, rather than of action.

*is "avoidance" the antidote to this*

2. **Loss of self:** Members of ACOA therapy groups are continually being invited to discard their unhealthy defenses. This request would be likely to cause some fear in any person. Yet ACOAs usually show even greater resistance. This resistance is present even when there is a stated desire to discard those defenses and coping mechanisms. It is based on a fear that *if they give up their defenses there will be nothing left.*

What does it mean to say there will be nothing left? It means that there is no true sense of self. ACOAs believe that people consist of what they *do*. ACOAs have used performance, taking care of others, and other externals to define themselves. Asking them to give up that external focus means that they must take the risk to be who they are. Paul is invited to be Paul—not a writer, worker, advocate, or business person. This is an enormous threat! It once again exposes the tension between yearning to be real and the fear of rejection.

This pursuit of self definition through externals signifies a belief that the person is essentially unlovable. It is a belief that people will only love ACOAs for what they do instead of who they are. There is no conception of being true to oneself. It is more a question of living up to (or in some

*compliance vs surrender*

*control vs abandon letting go*

*control vs abandon*

cases, thumbing their noses at) the perceived expectations of others.

An ACOA's control is attacked when group members' say his employment status isn't important to them. It is attacked when group members say they do not need favors from him. It is attacked when group members say they do not care what his criminal record is. Control is designed to keep the member's true self covered and thereby protected. His true self has been covered for so long that the person usually has no idea if it is still there—or ever was there to begin with!

3.  *Being overwhelmed.* Nowhere is control more evident than in the area of emotions. ACOAs fear that if they start expressing emotion such as anger and sorrow, they won't be able to stop. To do so would hurt someone or cause the walls to come tumbling down. They believe they will fall apart or be squashed by another person. The control is so evident that it is not unusual to see group members having physical reactions as they struggle to reign in their emotions.

ACOAs won't give in to joy because they believe it will be short lived. They won't share hurt because it may be used against them. They won't experience sorrow because the actions committed against them were justified. They won't express anger because they may be punished. They won't cry because tears mean they are weak. This is very hard work. It is also very lonely!

On an instinctive level, they know that there is enormous pressure inside of them from a lifetime of unresolved and unexpressed emotions. In one sense, there is no such thing as a simple emotion for them. The rage that explodes over a missed appointment has very little to do with that particular appointment. It comes from all the repressed emotion of the past festering inside.[2]

48

The ACOA is terrified of the dam shattering; he is aware of the stored-up force of those emotions. Control must be maintained at all costs or the person will be swept away in the deluge. This attempt at control results in even more repression, *and the vicious cycle continues!*

I am angry-
There is so much inside that if I express anger it will come out as rage-
I don't express the anger-

---

**Now there is even more inside of me!**

Control must be surrendered if the person is to become free. ACOA group therapy gives people a caring environment where they can dare to open the floodgates of emotion. They experience rage being expressed with no one being harmed. They experience deep sorrow and do not see people dissolve. They find that experiencing and expressing the repressed emotions results in freedom rather than in being overwhelmed. They find that rather than protecting them from repressed emotions, control has kept them in bondage to those very emotions.

## Control in Group Therapy

Sooner or later, every ACOA in group therapy must face the issue of control. The moment has many different faces, but it has the same underlying principles. That moment comes when ACOAs realize that *they are not in charge of their therapeutic process*. It is a realization that ACOA group therapy will not be done on their terms; they cannot control the process of the group. It strikes them with great force that *this is more than they bargained for!* It is precisely at this point that they either make a surrender to the recovery process or leave therapy.

49

1.  *Just as surrender versus compliance is an issue* in the treatment of acloholism,[3] it is also an issue in ACOA group therapy. Control is often manifested through compliance. A therapist should be on the lookout for group members who are too good to be true. (After all, this is one of the main symptoms of ACOAs.) These are the group members who are eager to look at everything that is discussed. In fact, they often seem prepared to bring up a subject and share about it in a meaningful way. They can be counted on to do a lot of confronting and expressing of emotion regarding what is happening in group.

After a period of time, some interesting insights become clear. *The member is always setting his own agenda regarding what will be shared.* After the member is done sharing, others have nothing to add because the person has dealt with everything. The member points out and acknowledges his own mistakes or faults before anyone else has a chance to. The member seems to be doing a lot of confronting and yet is rarely confronted. The group begins to look to the person for strength.

"What's wrong with that? It sounds good to me." Let's look at this a bit closer. It is revealing to see how our stalwart member reacts when it is pointed out that he never talks about spouse, job, sense of self, or dark fears. How does the person react to hearing that group members won't ask about those other areas because they are being kept busy with his agenda? Maybe someone will suggest that the person is using a *smoke screen* , which is a form of control, by offering select topics instead of ones which the individual is afraid to address.

*It is easier to share the presence of a defect, than the pain that defect causes* . We should look at the member's reaction when confronted on something he cannot see or didn't point out first. What happens when the group continues to confront the person on issues he has already admitted to? In acknowledging fault before anyone else, the person gives the group no easy place to go. It requires great courage for group members to say they will not settle for mere acknowledgment. *They expect and demand change.*

Because it is fairly easy to comply with the rules of ACOA group therapy, it can be done in such a manner as to preclude vulnerability in depth. It becomes a sharing only of what the person deems necessary. Lowering of defenses in some areas strengthens them in other, more vulnerable, ones. The person enters into relationships with others in order to control where that relationship will go.

*2. Control must be given up. Compliance is not enough .* Surrender is necessary. The terror of rejection and fear of being hurt must be faced, experienced, and shared. Surrender means people must give themselves to their fellow group members and place themselves in their hands.

Another area of control is the notion that ACOA group therapy is a luxury rather than a necessity. People come to group thinking they may have a few minor things they need to work on. They believe that all their present relationships are excellent. When pressed as to why they want to be in therapy, they give general answers. Their refusal to deal in specifics is usually a sign of control. There is an attitude (usually unacknowledged) that they are healthier than other group members. They are quick to praise other group members for the work they do. They tell fellow members of the progress they see in them. They express relief that their childhood was never *that* bad. In one sense they become detached observers or excited cheerleaders to the work of others.

*3. It is helpful to remind members that people who enter therapy are sick.* One does not join an ACOA therapy group because everything is going fine. Controllers generally leave therapy with statements such as, "I've worked hard to get where I am," "This is too negative," "You focus too much on problems," and "What good does it do to dredge up all this pain?" They refuse to look at their present relationships because at depth they are afraid of losing them. To admit that ACOA group therapy is a necessity is to admit that members are incapable of having healthy intimate relationships! This means that the relationships they have struggled so hard for may depend on their continued sickness.

Another type of control is shown by the group members who excel at playing "20 Questions." They are always there to help others get in touch with their feelings. They make great efforts to help others clarify what is going on by asking them questions. They are quick to share when they are confused or do not understand. In ACOA group therapy, most questions are used to avoid being honest with other members or to move out of the realm of experiencing emotions. "Are you mad?" is often used instead of, "I think you are mad." "Why did you do that?" is used to replace, "When you do that I feel...." "Are you sure you are sharing everything?" means, "I think you are holding something back." "Will we be talking about sex soon?" is another way of saying "I have a problem with sex I need to bring up in group."

When a member is struggling to express emotion or is attempting to avoid expressing emotions, it is quite common for the group to ask questions in order to "help". It is easier to ask questions to prod a resistant member along than it is to be honest with that member regarding his resistance. It is less threatening to say, "Does it have something to do with your mother?" than it is to say, "You seem to be fighting this and I'm tired of it." The person who is resisting is more than happy to play the question game rather than face the consequences of his resistance.

When a member is expressing deep emotions, asking questions allows other members to *keep the experience outside of themselves*. Instead of using the member's emotions as a key to unlock their own, they use questions to keep the focus on the other person. The questioning allows the other members to respond to the expression of honest deep emotion from an intellectual standpoint. *The questions attempt to clarify an event rather than share an experience.*

Questions usually get an intellectual response. They involve little risk. They are an excellent means of control since they often allow points to be made with little vulnerability. Once we enter the realm of understanding, we can share our thoughts rather than our emotions.

One of the all-time methods of control found in ACOAs can be summed up in the phrases, "What should I be feeling?" and, "What do you want me to do?" A good rule of thumb is to realize that *these are not questions in the true sense.* They are usually said out of anger and can generally be viewed as an attack. They are an attempt to shift responsibility to the other person. There is no acknowledgment that the members need to take a risk or examine themselves. This indicates no real attempt to share at depth. Once again ACOAs are adapting to an external environment instead of sharing who they are. It would be a lot more honest for them to say, "I feel numb and I am withdrawing," or, "I am afraid to do anything".

A member's on-going efforts to "play therapist" are also attempts to control. This usually shows itself as a member's analyzing other members' statements. He acts as interpreter, one time explaining what the therapist is saying, and another time acting as the ombudsman for the group. The member's efforts in group are on a very intellectual level. The member wants to understand everything and have the process of recovery explained. He questions the therapist's competence and also questions the techniques that are used.

It is important to stop at this point and make a crucial distinction. It is not wrong to question and criticize. It is, however, unhealthy to question or criticize in group *without sharing emotions as well* . During play therapy it is not appropriate to say, "I don't see why we are doing this." It is, however, very appropriate to say, "I feel silly", "I don't want to let myself go", or, "I've never done this and I don't know how." During art therapy it is not appropriate to say, "This is a waste of time. I don't think we should be doing this." It is very appropriate to say, "I'm afraid to draw", "I'm embarrassed at my drawing skills", "I don't know how to start." When clients act as therapist or critic, they are attempting to control their own therapy. They share little of themselves and set themselves apart from other members.

4.  *Control is insidious throughout ACOA group therapy* . The therapist must be continually alert for it and develop a variety of approaches to it. There is no particular method for dealing with control. The kind of technique that may be necessary to confront the person playing therapist, may not work for the member who is

struggling to control tears. At times the therapist must step in, and yet at others, the therapist should wait for the group to address the issue. It is important to remember that control has been developed in ACOAs as a means to survival. It has been developed as a response to an unreasonable environment. Therefore, it is not a question of fault or blame. The message must be continually communicated that just because the behavior is inappropriate, it does not mean that the person is unlovable. It must also be made clear to the ACOA that although his behavior may be designed to keep people away, the therapist and group members will continue to accept him while rejecting his behavior. An invitation to be real is being offered and an honest, open environment is being created.

*"Happiness is relief from pressure."*

*"I'm not defensive. I'm defiant."*

*"Me and my mind were getting along just fine."*

*"The old way was painful, but at least I knew how it worked."*

*"I'm constantly on the run so all my fears are combined in this huge fear of slowing down."*

*"I wouldn't do anything because I was waiting to see how things worked out."*

*"I want to come and learn the right thing to do without telling anyone and then go home and fix it by myself."*

*"I had a hell of a week but I'm all jolly in time for group."*

*"Quick get-aways are my style — the quicker the better."*

# VII. SEPARATION

## Who Was That Masked Man?

### Importance of Separation

One of the main issues an ACOA therapy group must face is separation. The group will be confronted with separation almost from the very beginning. People leave treatment in a variety of ways, most of which are unhealthy. Before we can examine separation in the context of group therapy, we must examine separation and leave-taking in the life of the ACOA. Once again, we will see the issues of trust, intimacy, control, and fear play major roles. Initially ACOAs handle departure in group the same way they do outside of therapy. One function of group therapy is to provide them with a laboratory to learn how to separate in a healthy, feeling manner.

# Methods of Separation

The common theme which is found in the many ways ACOAs deal with ending a relationship is *the avoidance of legitimate pain.*[1] Pain occurs in healthy separation. It results from addressing the reality of the relationship and the emotions that changing it produces. Any particular leave-taking must be viewed against a mosaic of guarded emotions, rationalizations, repressed expectations and unexpressed needs.

The following are some of the ways ACOAs deal with separation. Though these methods are not unique to this population, the depth of their roots in ACOAs makes them easily identifiable components of their defense systems.

## 1. Silence
Once a person announces he is leaving, *the subject is never discussed!* That is not to say there is no talking. There is a lot of talk regarding the new home, the new job, how hard packing is, what the weather will be like, or anything else that has to do with the situation. What is missing is any talk about the separation itself. No one mentions the pain. No one talks about the fear of making new friends or the fear that there will never be another intimate relationship.

## 2. Absence
The best way to avoid saying goodbye is to not be present when someone is departing. An easy way to leave a relationship is simply not to return. Both of these methods preclude the possibility of sharing with another person. They are essentially self-centered in that they deny the reality of other people by not recognizing them or their needs. Absence is generally justified through excuses such as having already said goodbye, having other commitments, not wanting to put the other person in pain, and claiming there is nothing left to say.

### 3. Tight schedule

The tight schedule is a cousin to absence. This allows the ACOA to fulfill the conventions of separation yet not have to feel the pain. The person can usually only "break away" for a couple of minutes to say goodbye. As if by coincidence the person generally arrives while some commotion is going on (i.e., dinner, packing, moving). Everything about the person says he can't stay (i.e., the car may be left running, he remains standing while everyone's sitting, he leaves his coat on). This invitation to superficiality allows the task to be accomplished while the pain is not embraced.

### 4. Smile and get away

This method can be adapted by both extroverts and introverts. The extrovert addresses the departure with a handshake and a big smile. The extrovert exudes confidence. This method also precludes the possibility of mutual sharing because the person appears to be in such control. The introvert, however, accepts the topic being brought up by others. He looks shy, smiles a lot, and doesn't say too much. There is no mutual sharing because the introvert becomes a receiver who returns little to the other people.

### 5. I'm so happy...

This method takes two forms. The first is, "I'm so happy for you...." The people who remain talk about how happy they are that their departing friend has such a great opportunity ahead. They become cheerleaders and spend a lot of time telling the person how lucky he is. It would not be right to express pain or sorrow regarding the departure. That would be ruining it. In one sense ACOAs find it easier to admit to jealousy regarding the person's opportunity rather than admitting to the pain regarding their friend's leaving. Instead, the focus is on the future. The emotions of the present are never fully shared.

The second form is, "I'm so happy to have this opportunity." The person leaving never addresses the pain of departure because the focus is on the future. It is as if the present does not exist. It becomes a period of waiting rather than a period of living. Though the person is still present physically, he is already gone from the relationship.

## 6. Emotional fade-out

"The lights are on but nobody's home" is a good way to describe this. Once separation is on the horizon, there is a withdrawal. The same amount of time may be spent together, but withdrawal has begun. The people begin to fade into themselves. This is different than preparing for departure. In a healthy relationship separation is dealt with openly and becomes a joint process. The people, through sharing emotions, actually come closer. The emotional fade-out of ACOAs is a solitary venture which often is at odds with their physical actions.

## 7. The Scarlet O'Hara

"I'll think about it tomorrow" characterizes this method. There are so many things to do in order to prepare for departure that there is no time to experience emotions. Separation becomes a series of tasks one must move through at a rapid pace. It involves a lot of energy and planning. It is a very busy process. Another variation of this is the avoidance of *any* action. Life goes on as if nothing is going to happen. No plans are made. Relationships are treated as if they will stay the same. Separation occurs by default. After the person leaves there will be time to deal with the relationship! There will be plans to write letters in order to "really" say goodbye once the departed person has settled. It generally doesn't happen.

## 8. Picking a fight

Is there any better way to avoid the pain of separation than by having a fight? Not only does it take the ACOA through the actual departure, but a well-nursed resentment can last for weeks, making the separation a remote event in the past. The fight is usually a dishonest way of expressing the emotions generated by the separation. It precludes vulnerability by going on the attack. It provides the person with numerous reasons why he shouldn't feel bad. After all, now that the other person's true colors are shown, the departing member is actually glad to be rid of him! Once again a mechanism has been found to prevent feeling and the honest expression of emotions.

## 9. Finding fault

This is a more subtle version of picking a fight. It can be used by a person having to rationalize the decision and limit the pain of departure. It can also be used by those who remain, as a reason not to feel emotion. The more faults that can be found, the less necessary it is to feel sad about the separation. This is a subtle process that takes place over a period of time. It involves a shift in perspective. Rather than being a vehicle for mutual creation, the relationship becomes something which a person stands outside of and criticizes. The person using this method disclaims any responsibility for on-going growth and change in the relationship. Instead, the person reacts based on self-centeredness.

## 10. Leaving upon arrival

ACOAs begin steeling themselves for a person's departure at approximately the same time a person enters their lives. They won't be needy so they won't be hurt at separation, or they'll be super needy so the person will have to stay. Their actions are calculated not to drive the person away. They continually try to impress or earn their way. They portray a studied nonchalance about the relationship in order not to scare the person away or to appear invulnerable to emotional blackmail. ACOAs believe that ultimately they are on their own. As a result of this belief, they try not to get their hopes up regarding a relationship.

\* \* \*

Separation means a change in relationships. Relationships involve people. People involve emotions. For our purposes, separation is from people, not from situations. Departure is from people, not from a place. An ACOA does not depart group therapy; he separates from the members of the group. The group members who remain have had someone leave them. The decision is not merely to separate. The decision is to change a person's relationship with others. It is precisely this recognition—that *separation involves altering relationships with other feeling human beings*—which must be made in ACOA group therapy. *It turns separation from a task which must be dealt with to an opportunity for intimacy*. It can become one of the healthiest of human interactions. For this reason it is of *crucial importance* to the ACOA therapy group.

## Methods of Leaving Group

It will be helpful to explore some of the unhealthy ways members have left ACOA group therapy. They generally take the form of an announcement. Group members are denied the opportunity to enter their decision making process. Along with this denial, there is a defensiveness and abruptness. It is as if they are preparing for an attack and want to make a quick escape. There is also a rigidity and tightness to the explanation (if one is offered). It shows that the member must have been thinking about leaving for some time. "QED" is all that is missing from his closing statement. There is no room for discussion, and the member takes the stance of defending a decision rather than exploring alternatives.

1. **The letter**
   Mailing the therapist a letter is a popular way for an ACOA to leave group therapy. These letters show a richness of pathology that provides fuel for discussion for the next three sessions. Within these letters can be found the core material for a seminar on ACOA symptoms!

# "Letter #1

*Just a brief note to let you know I am still surviving amidst much confusion and conflict. I will not waste your time by going into a multitude of words and lengthy explanations for my lack of attendance at the Adult Children's group, but just state the facts as they are. I will not be returning because:*
*1. I have been in more conflict and pain than I like.*
*2. I firmly feel 90% of my particular problems lie not only in myself but also a real communication gap with my spouse and myself.* This we are consciously working on.
*3. Due to some of my experiences and dealings with people,* I no longer want to share my innermost self, *because other than "The Group Experience," people are limited and fallible and a price is paid by vulnerable people like myself that* I choose to avoid at least for the present time.
*4. I intend to focus more of my attention on the people who really do love me and care about me. That is my immediate family. My priorities I have discovered are completely out of whack.*

*Thanks for the privilege of your company if for only a brief time. I have attained one goal: I must trust and love myself first before I can try to please others. I have begun to do this and through the grace of God and support of my family "I will overcome".*

This letter shows that a choice has been made between the process of recovery and self-sufficiency. A decision has been made to back away from the pain that must be experienced if one is to be free. It is very revealing that the person does not want to share his "innermost self." It is very understandable as well as very sad.

It is painful to think of the turmoil and solitude this letter reflects. This person came into therapy looking for an answer and is now confused and scared by the pain recovery entails. Since the person never brought this up in group, there was no chance for healing or reassurance. Here is a person with enormous good will trying to

61

confused and scared by the pain recovery entails. Since the person never brought this up in group, there was no chance for healing or reassurance. Here is a person with enormous good will trying to build communication and intimacy by conscious hard work without a foundation to build upon. The lonely swim upstream continues.

## Letter #2

*Hi! Hope you're having a good day!*

*After much reflection, prayer, and discussion with sponsors, I have decided not to continue in group therapy. I did enjoy my introduction to the group, but do not feel it's a particularly good or necessary place for me to be. I do hope we can share experience and knowledge as professionals in the future.*

*Thanks for your interest and caring!*

This letter reflects a decision based upon reflection, prayer, and discussion with others, but no involvement with fellow group members. Group members were avoided because they, in all probability, would give the person a response he does not want to hear. The letter is so tightly structured that it allows for no response to the decision itself. Since it also reveals no reasons for the action, there is no room for personal interaction or intimacy. It is easier to share "as professionals" than as people!

## Letter #3

*I'm letting you know that I've decided to leave group. I care for you all very much. This is a choice that's right for me and one that's comfortable for me today.*

This letter was written by a person who was a member of an ACOA therapy group for almost a year. It shows no acknowledgement *of any relationship!* The person viewed therapy not as the establishment of a community but as something to be attended. There is no recognition that this "choice" affected others. "Me" appears to be the key word. It shows a self-centeredness that is defiant as well as defensive.

It is not being argued that this person should not leave or should not make decisions based upon a perception of his best interest. The point is that *the person was living a lie in group* . This member's presence indicated belonging and commitment, and yet the person walked out of the other people's lives without saying goodbye. This person shared neither process nor self with other group members. The decision itself is not as important as how it is made and how it is shared.

## Letter #4

*I will no longer be coming to group. Thank you for your services.*

Would you like to be this person? What must be going on inside someone to leave group in such a manner after attending for eight months? Once the decision to leave was made, it seems the fellow group members not only ceased to exist but never existed to begin with. There was a lot of risk-taking, vulnerability, joy, and sorrow during the eight months. People, no matter how fumbling, tentative, or awkward, attempted to let others into their lives. To dismiss this with "Thank you for your services," shows control at its most extreme.

## Letter #5

*I have made a decision to drop out of group and continue treatment elsewhere. I would like to thank you for the time and help that you have given me. At the present time I feel there is more that I can gain by seeking treatment elsewhere. I will continue to talk to group members individually about my decision, as I feel this will be a healthier way for me to separate.*

*Again thank you.*

This person had promised group members to attend three sessions after a decision to leave was made. This would allow time to process separation and leave in a healthy manner. Instead, this letter was received two weeks after the member had ceased attending group. The problem is not the decision to leave, it is the broken promise that was made to other group members.

The person has decided "to talk to other group members individually about my decision," because "I feel this will be a healthier way for me to separate". Why do you think this decision was made? A great response from one group member was, "It's easier to get away with our old tricks with one person than it is to pull them over on ten people." In announcing the decision to one person, it is fairly easy to control the conversation and dictate what will be discussed. It is not "healthier." It is, however, less threatening and more controlling. The person does not have to let the other group members into his life. The member simply informs them of this unilateral action which will alter their relationship.

## Letter #6

*This letter is to notify you that I have decided to terminate my affiliation with group and individual counseling.*

*I want to thank you for your support and help. It has been a valuable experience; one that I will continue to build on. At this time, however, I feel that the work I need to do can best be done elsewhere. I am continuing to receive counseling.*

*I will always be grateful for the time and work I have done at your agency.*

64

This letter has everything. It expresses gratitude, indicates intentions to pursue counseling, and a desire to build on a "valuable experience." Despite all of these qualities, it is also very hollow. Coupled with the nice words is a coldness. A healthy person does not use the method of notification to leave an intimate relationship. "Terminate my affiliation" does not reflect the reality of the action taken. It is an attempt to numb the pain and deny the reality of the relationships which have been left.

## 2. The bombshell

This takes the form of an announcement which is proclaimed ten minutes before the end of group. It is usually preceded by the words, "Oh, by the way." It informs group members of a decision that has already been made. There is no place for participation by other members; they are presented with an accomplished fact

The other members are not viewed as caring, concerned people, but become opponents instead. The task changes from mutual exploration to a tenacious battle to defend a decision. The member is generally well controlled in the ensuing struggle. The announcement is made casually, and followed by silence. The protective shield goes up, and no one can penetrate it. The member may respond briefly to questions but there is no openness. The storm only has to be weathered for another seven minutes, and then he will be free. It is no coincidence that the announcement comes at the end of the session!

When people use the bombshell, they are generally caught between two worlds. One part wants to leave and not say goodbye. Another part wants to say goodbye, but doesn't know how. They are not able to commit themselves to a course of action. In one sense this mirrors their participation in therapy. It is the yearning for intimacy coupled with the terror of it. The result is a state of turmoil which has them seeking relationships and then turning away when intimacy begins to develop.

3. The fade-away
Many times ACOAs leave group therapy but forget to tell their bodies. They remain physically present, yet they are very removed. It is fairly easy to spot when the withdrawal began. It can generally be traced to a confrontation, a painful issue, or an instance of the person's own deep sharing. Whatever the reason, the decision has been made. Though the member does not verbalize it, the decision is obvious. The physical appearance changes, there is little eye contact, and no appropriate response to questions. The member claims nothing is going on and sits very still. The path of least resistance has been taken. Aware of the confrontation that the departure will trigger, the member remains silent. Group becomes something which is merely attended. A tremendous disservice is done in staying. Once again an ACOA is acting to avoid conflict or win approval while resenting it the whole time.

The key to the fade-away is to find an excuse to leave physically. This excuse must be external. Finances are often used, as are schedules, bowling leagues, and distances to be traveled. A classic quote for this case is, *"They dumped on me for not participating, so it's better for me to leave so I won't hold the group back."* Do not underestimate how patient the member will be in waiting for the excuse! It is easier to have other people be responsible than to assume personal responsibility.

4. **The attack**
Essential to the attack is the belief that a particular member has more insight than other group members. The member justifies departing by criticizing what is happening. The unspoken message is, "If you had any brains, you would leave as well." It is an attempt to characterize the ACOA therapy group, which the person has been a part of, as irrelevant at best and harmful at worst. The attack diverts the focus of attention. It seeks to provoke a discussion of the agency and the therapeutic process instead of the member's own participation and level of recovery.

The attack can be focused on the group members: "My problems are different", "You don't call me up", "I wouldn't choose to socialize with you", "We have nothing in common", or "You let the therapist control you." It also can be focused on the process: "All this is dredging up the past", "You're trying to make problems where there are none", and "Al-Anon is all we really need to deal with this". The most common, however, is the attack on the therapist.

A member in a group for nine months will decide to leave and not say goodbye because of a problem with the therapist: "The therapists cause too much pain", "The therapists don't share enough of themselves", "They won't answer my questions", or "My issues aren't being addressed". These are all reasons people have used for leaving. Some, or all, of these reasons may be true. The therapist may have made errors. The pathology is that *no attempt is made by the ACOA to resolve the problems in a direct manner* . The perceived problems have been mulled over outside of group where they can only fester. In one sense, the departing member has a vested interest in having them remain unresolved. The best defense is a good offense!

## How Groups Respond

A lot can be learned from how the group members respond when a person departs in one of the above manners. The therapist can be sure that it produces a profound effect. *This may not be visible* and may even be denied by certain members, but is there nevertheless.

1.  The first reaction is silence. It is not a peaceful silence. Tension fills the room. It is important for the therapist to note, and later return to, the physical appearances and sensations of the group members. Veins pop and jaws work. Some people fidget while others remain frozen. Some faces

are deadpan and rigid, and others strain to keep emotion inside. It does the group members a disservice if the therapist interrupts the silence and dissipates the tension.

2. Now the questions and the attempts to convince come. "Do you really think you're ready?", "Have you really done your best?", "You just said last month how much you needed to be here." The group members attempt to understand why the member is leaving, while the departing member gives guarded explanations. The group members attempt to convince the departing member to stay but he doesn't respond. It becomes very similar to a debate with one side attempting to score points and the other providing minimal response.

3. Anger is next to enter the scene. Some members are able to say they are mad at the person for leaving. However, sometimes there is a twist to it. "I am mad because you are leaving and not giving yourself a chance to get better." "I am mad because I think you are fooling yourself." The anger is because the person is passing up a chance for self-improvement. The anger is because the person remains unconvinced despite the eloquence and persuasiveness of the group's arguments.

Now the rest of the members express anger—but not to the departing member! They focus on the other members who are trying to change the person's mind. The group starts to fight among itself. Other group members now become advocates and interpreters for the departing member. They do not view the person's leaving as a "big deal." They claim the person's decision to leave is a personal decision and has no effect on them. "We should support the decision." "People know what's best for themselves." "Who are we to judge?" "Departure is hard enough." These members do not want to make the situation worse by adding conflict to it.

The departing member now gets mad because, "I'm getting tired of you dumping on me." Everyone is mad at one thing or another. It confirms the member's decision to leave. "These people really don't understand after all, and they probably intend to stay in group the rest of their lives." The person actually leaves with a sense of relief.

4.  At this point in the chaos comes the "Let's move on" stage. There appears to be no way of resolving the situation and somebody brings up another topic. "If we are done with this, I'd like to talk about...." There is a desire to get out of the room, or at least change the subject. This is not an attempt to put the past behind. *It is an attempt to repress the present and act as if it never existed!*

The session after a person departs suddenly (or the session a letter is received) is fun for the therapist. There is a lot to review and share regarding the departure. Members will have spent a great deal of their time thinking about, or attempting to ignore, the departure. Exploring physical sensations members had the previous week, unresolved anger, guilt, fear for themselves, and fears for the future of the group make the time fly. Members can address how this will affect their future participation and sharing. A person's abrupt departure can be a tremendous gift for the remaining members because it opens the door to a lot of fears, emotions, and memories.

# A Quiz

THIS IS A TEST! *What is missing from the four steps the group took to deal with the separation?* If you did not answer that there was no sharing of self or vulnerability on the part of the remaining members, then stop here and re-read this book!

The members' efforts were all directed outside of themselves. No one focused on how the person's departure hurt them. The members did not share the pain they felt having someone leave their lives. No one expressed anger about being written off by the person who left.

## As the Group Gets Healthy

As an ACOA therapy group gets healthy, its members start to make appropriate demands of each other. They go against the lessons of their past and begin to have expectations of others. They demand honesty. Fellow group members are expected to share themselves. A vulnerability is developed which allows others into their lives. They begin to depend on the fact that group members will be there for them. A community or family is being created based on trust, intimacy, and vulnerability.

In ACOA group therapy, people are touched at depth by other members. They have taken great risks and shared deeply. They come to realize that risk, trust, and acceptance are part of the healing process. When people leave group in an unhealthy way, they are breaking this bond in a callous manner. They are slamming the door on a relationship. This is the key to the group's response. It is easier to question a decision than to admit pain. It is safer to claim no expectations than to admit vulnerability and hurt. Concern for others conceals concern for self. A turning point is reached when a person can say to a departing member, "I am hurt and furious because you are leaving my life without involving me," instead of, "I feel bad that you didn't give the group a chance."

## Gifts of Separation

1. Group members have an opportunity to be honest about their feelings. They are actually pushed to be real. They do not have to say the right thing or feel the correct way. The separation must be addressed. It cannot be ignored.

2. Perhaps for the first time, group members can experience a separation. They are physically present and called upon to

process it. During that process they tap the pain of many previous separations that have never been addressed. They can use this as an opportunity to experience the pain they have been afraid to look at. It also shows them the depth of both their hurt and the task ahead of them.

3. They can see that they are not alone. All ACOAs have been hurt by separation, either physical or emotional. As other members share the pain of previous separations, a closer community is created. Attempting to deny it only creates more isolation.

4. Group members learn a valuable lesson. A person has left. It is painful, but it's not the end of the world. A person has left, causing great pain, and no one has died. The very thing ACOAs have been terrified of has happened, and they have survived. In fact they have done more than survive. They have used it as an opportunity to grow.

5. Group members have experienced that being vulnerable and trying to love involve pain. They have seen that trusting people involves disappointment. They now have an opportunity to say "Yes" to life. They must choose between safety with its slow decay, or life with its richness. A tremendous moment has been born from the pain of rejection!

*"Once again someone who I have opened myself up to is leaving."*

*"You're taking yourself from me and there is nothing I can do about it."*

*"I didn't really need to be here anyway."*

*"This is not for me. I need to get on with my life."*

*"I'm sick of alcoholism. I won't let it be the
center of my life."*

*"So, he's not going to be here anymore. Let's
move on, it's no big deal."*

*"What's the use?"*

*"A person I love has left and I'm powerless."*

*"I'm pissed off because I'm still here! You probably expect people to be in group forever."*

# VIII.  EVALUATION AND DEPARTURE

## The Road Worth Traveling

Sometimes it is so easy to focus on unhealthy separation that we forget about preparing for a healthy departure. We spend so much time pointing out why people should remain in ACOA group therapy that the criteria for departure do not get addressed. When is it time for a group member to depart? Is there an evaluation process which can be applied to all group members? These questions must be answered in order to give ACOAs a sense of their place in the recovery process and specific goals to strive for in therapy.

## Evaluation

The evaluation process in ACOA group therapy does not consist of a therapist grading a group member's performance. Evaluation is not something which can be external to the therapeutic process. It is a valuable tool which not only measures people's progress but can be used to help them obtain their goals in recovery. Evaluation is an on-going procedure in which the group member, fellow group members, and therapist share and explore the individual's journey during group. Not only does it bring people more self-awareness, it also brings them closer to others.

## Self-Assessment

It is important that group members evaluate their progress on a weekly basis. Such evaluation is difficult to focus. To address this problem we have decided to examine one particular area: the member's participation during the weekly therapy session. The assumption is that a member's participation in ACOA group therapy reflects his functioning outside of group.

Each group member is given an evaluation form after each session. The form asks questions which fall into the categories of relationships, emotions and self-awareness. This process must be viewed as an integral part of therapy. The members are expected to write their answers and be very specific. Being required to give written evaluations of their activity during group has affected their performance. Members are more hesitant to remain silent and act as observers, because evaluation removes the element of safety they may have sought in their silence. Through this process of self-evaluation, they must address who they are and what their relationship is with their fellow group members. It becomes more difficult to slide through group.

## 1. The Self-Evaluation Form

The self-evaluation form is comprised of three categories. There are a total of twelve questions to which the group member must provide written answers. A form is completed each week.

## Relationships

These questions are designed to examine what the member did to form relationships during group. They give the members insight into the nature of their relationship, allowing them to explore their level of honesty and degree of commitment to their fellow members. Members can see how they attempt to define relationships and operate within them.

1. Was I honest with group members about what I saw in their behavior? If yes, how? If no, why not?

2. Was I honest with group members about how I felt toward them? If yes, how? If no, why not?

3. How did I let people into my life during group? If I did not, why not?

## Emotions

This section deals with emotions on two levels: identification and sharing. Emotions become legitimate topics of inquiry rather than something to be ignored. If a member is claiming not to have emotion or is repressing emotion, then these are issues to be addressed. The process of evaluation gives emotions a legitimacy and presence which can't comfortably be ignored.

4. What emotions did I identify during group?

5. What emotions did I express directly during group?


6. Did I use telling a story, giving an analysis, saying I don't know, or questions of clarification to hide what I was really feeling?


7. When was I afraid to share my feelings?


## Self-awareness

This section is designed to give members an opportunity to explore who they are. It begins to help them develop a sense of identity. They can see themselves as people rather than performers. They get a sense of their own complexity. Recovery becomes a process rather than an all or nothing affair. They can gently assess where they are and set modest goals as to where they wish to be.


8. What defenses did I use during group?


9. What risks did I take?


10. What was I afraid to look at during group?


11. What am I most proud of about myself during group?

12. What are my goals for next week's group?


## Evaluation by Group Members

It is characteristic of ACOAs to make assessments of themselves in a vacuum. That is one of the reasons group therapy is the treatment of choice for this population. Through this special relationship, members can learn how others view them and how their behavior affects others. Done in an open and honest manner, this evaluation avoids innuendo, hints and unspoken signals. Both parties, by conscious decision, enter into the process of awareness and revelation.

Participation in ACOA group therapy is in itself an on-going evaluation. Through confrontation and sharing emotions, members learn not only how another sees them, but how their behavior affects others. They experience that they are not solitary agents acting in isolation. Their behavior can and does have an influence on relationships. Members not only have the opportunity to open or close themselves to others, but through confrontation and feedback they can see whether a particular behavior aids or hinders their efforts.

Members must be given the opportunity to share their self-evaluations during group. This can be done when requested by a member or on a sporadic basis by the therapist. While self-evaluation is useful, it becomes much more meaningful if it is shared with fellow group members in a structured setting. The very act of sharing is a lessening of control and taking of a risk. It is a step toward intimacy. It is an invitation to grow together.

Often an ACOA's perception of self is different from the perception held by others. It is not unusual for ACOAs to discover that their beliefs regarding another's perception were mistaken. Peer review of the self-evaluation enables perceptions and assumptions to be validated or discarded. It brings everyone closer to reality.

It is important for members to hear how their lack of honesty affected others. Members need to know how taking risks affected their relationships with others. Other members need to share with the individual how the person's expression of emotion triggered something in themselves. In a real way members are becoming accountable to each other. As members of an ACOA therapy group, people are expected to share themselves. They have become members of a community. A lack of interaction will not be ignored. This self-evaluation and group review often bring fear to group members for that very reason. It becomes very difficult for them to hide in group.

## Therapist Evaluation

It is important that the therapist monitor each member's progress (or lack of progress). Unless the therapist does this, some members will become invisible and lost. It is easy to focus on the more verbal members while ignoring the silent ones. A lack of evaluation will cause the therapy group to become unfocused. The group as a unit will begin to drift and members lose sight of their objectives. They begin to think group will last forever.

## 1. Weekly Evaluation

After each session the therapist completes an evaluation checklist for each group member. This allows the therapist not only to evaluate the member's participation in a given session, but to develop a history of the group member's journey. It forces the therapist to take into consideration each individual group member. It ensures that no one will be ignored. If the therapist is forced to account for a member's continued lack of participation, it is safe then to assume the member will be forced to address it as well.

The following is an example of the weekly evaluation checklist:

# WEEKLY EVALUATION CHART

| Name | Partici pation | Selfrev- elation | Identify and Express Emotions | Relation- ships | Risks Taken | Comments |
|------|---------------|------------------|-------------------------------|-----------------|-------------|----------|
|      |               |                  |                               |                 |             |          |
|      |               |                  |                               |                 |             |          |
|      |               |                  |                               |                 |             |          |

Scale of 1 to 4:

4   Excellent
3   Good

2   Needs Improvement
1   Poor

The checklist attempts to record a member's efforts in the categories necessary for recovery. The therapist, through assignments, topics of discussion, and appropriate confrontations, can make adjustments to address the needs of individuals. The group ceases to be an indivisible unit and becomes composed of unique individuals with similar but varying needs.

## 2. Quarterly Evaluation

Individual therapy sessions for the purposes of evaluation are essential for both group members and the therapist. They provide an opportunity for an in-depth examination of members' progress. The members and the therapist can evaluate which goals have been obtained, which ones need more work, and whether new goals are necessary. These sessions are not only concerned with where the members are going, but how they can get there.

Every three months the member meets with the therapist to review his participation in group as well as his growth outside of group. The therapist can see how the member has internalized the lessons learned. It is important to deal in specifics and to be concrete. It is not enough to learn that a member's relationship with his/her spouse has improved. How it has improved, what it feels like, and how the member will work to continue the improvement must be examined.

It is useful at this session to go over the self-evaluation and weekly checklist. They are visible reminders of the work done in the previous quarter. It aids in setting realistic and attainable goals. *Members can see the evolution of their recovery.* Setting the short-term goal of letting fellow members know when a person is afraid will aid in the attainment of the long-term goal of intimacy. These sessions serve as a road map to attainment of the long term-goals of recovery. *The method of attaining goals must be given the same importance as the goals themselves.*

# Departure

## Tasks

Evaluation presupposes departure. ACOAs need not be in therapy forever. It is essential to realize that ACOA group therapy is not an end in itself. It is also not recovery itself. It is a vehicle for recovery. A member's journey in group has a beginning, middle, and the potential for a healthy end.

Members' recovery through ACOA group therapy is full of paradoxes. Members are not ready for independence until they acknowledge and embrace their dependence on the group. Members cannot take control of their lives in a healthy way until they have first given up control absolutely. It is death and resurrection. Victory through surrender.

It is fairly easy to create a checklist of tasks which must be accomplished to indicate the completion of a member's time in therapy:

-a remembrance and experience of the past
-mourning the past
-discovery and acceptance of self
-the sharing of self through vulnerability
-coming alive emotionally
-letting others into the process of their lives
-developing needs and allowing others to care for them
-forming relationships based on honesty, vulnerability, shared
    emotion and risk-taking

However, these are more than tasks. They don't happen sequentially. They represent the process of *a person coming alive*.

## Art Rather Than Science

You may be thinking that you have been given very little objective criteria for departure. You are right. The checklist will give some guidelines, but the area of departure is closer to an art than a science. Healthy departure is the result of an on-going process. It is the concresence of a member's recovery.

The signature of a healthy departure is openness. There is a willingness to involve group members in the decision. The process involves not only making a decision, but embracing and sharing the emotions that go with it. As with birth, there is pain, but there is great joy and happiness as well. There is a lot of crying, laughing and sharing. A person who has come of age is being given a send-off by a loving family. The moment is full of *life and nurturance!* How different from the letter, the bombshell, the fade-away, and the attack. It represents the evolution of a relationship rather than the termination of one.

Absence of pain, total intimacy, conquering fear and absolute resolution of issues are *not* criteria for departure. If they were, no one would ever leave therapy! The pursuit of these criteria would also further ACOAs' quest for perfection and foster their all-or-nothing mentality. Instead, we look for a member's consistent and progressive ability to be *real and spontaneous* . The recovery process is based on acceptance of both self and others as feeling, vulnerable human beings. It is the ability to have relationships based on freedom and openness, rather than fear and manipulation. When a person can be who he or she truly is—viewing the past with freedom and forgiveness, and willing to take the risks intimacy and vulnerability entail—then it is time to depart.

A member's departure as a result of this shared process must be celebrated. Group members must be given the opportunity to experience the pain as well as share in the joy and excitement. In this manner, a member who has departed still remains with the group as the group remains within the departing member.

*"I'm hurting because I'm leaving group but I'm so happy that I didn't leave group because I hurt."*

# IX.  CONCLUSION

## Onward!

The issue of treatment for ACOAs must be addressed. This book has been an attempt to show one therapist's approach, group therapy, and some areas for exploration. In the introduction I invited you to take what this book has to offer, and filter it through your own experience and insight. Sharing and expanding upon existing knowledge are the methods by which treatment is developed and refined.

The alarm has already been sounded. More and more people have been alerted to the plight of ACOAs. While we continually work to carry the message, equal effort must be given in developing effective therapy. The debate *whether* ACOAs need help is over. The debate regarding the best treatment modality is just beginning!

*Paul  Curtin,  MA,  CAC*
*Syracuse,  New  York*
*1985*

83

# X. I AM AN ADULT WHO GREW UP IN AN ALCOHOLIC FAMILY*

Here are some of the things I found out about myself and that I am now beginning to change:

1. I guess at what normal is.
2. I have difficulty following projects through from beginning to end.
3. I lie when it would be just as easy to tell the truth.
4. I judge myself without mercy.
5. I have difficulty having fun.
6. I take myself very seriously.
7. I have difficulty with intimate relationships.
8. I overreact to changes over which I have no control.
9. I feel different from other people.
10. I constantly seek approval and affirmation.
11. I am either super responsible or super irresponsible.
12. I am extremely loyal even in the face of evidence that the loyalty is undeserved.
13. I look for immediate, as opposed to deferred, gratification.

---

* Reprinted with permission: Copyright © 1983 by Thomas W. Perrin, Inc., P.O. Box 190, Rutherford, NJ 07070

14. I lock myself into a course of action without giving serious consideration to alternate behaviors or possible consequences.
15. I seek tension and crisis and then complain about the results.
16. I avoid conflict or aggravate it; rarely do I deal with it.
17. I fear rejection and abandonment, yet I am rejecting of others.
18. I fear failure, but sabotage my success.
19. I fear criticism and judgment, yet I criticize and judge others.
20. I manage my time poorly and do not set my priorities in a way that works out well for me.


I have survived against impossible odds until today. With the help of God and my friends, I shall survive the next twenty-four hours. I am no longer alone.

# REFERENCES

## Introduction

1. NACOA, P.O. Box 42116691, San Francisco, California 941142
2. NYSCOAF, P.O. Box 9, Hempstead, New York 11550
3. Black, C., *It Will Never Happen to Me*, Medical Administration Co., Denver. CO, 1982.
4. Woititz, J., *Adult Children of Alcoholics*, Health Communications, Inc., Hollywood, Florida, 1983.
5. Wegscheider, S., *Another Chance: Hope and Health for the Alcoholic Family*, Science and Behavior Books, Palo Alto, California, 1981.
6. Black, C., Presentation at Children of Alcoholics: A National Perspective Conference, March 8, 1984, New York.

## Group Therapy

1. Wegscheider, S., "Another Chance" (film), Health Communication, Inc., Hollywood, Florida, 1983.
2. Brown, S., Presentation, NYS Coalition for Children of Alcoholic Families Conference, October, 1984.

3. Royce, J., *Alcohol Problems and Alcoholism: A comprehensive Survey*, The Free Press, 1981, p. 269.
4. Gorski, T., and Miller, *Counseling for Relapse Prevention* , Independence Press, Independence, Missouri, 1979.


## Relationships

1. Johnson, V., *I'll Quit Tomorrow*, Harper and Row, Publishers, San Francisco, California, 1980, p. 43.


## Emotions

1. Perrin, T., *COA Review* , No. 5, Thomas Perrin, Inc., Rutherford, New Jersey, September/October, 1983.


## Control

1. Cermak, T., and Brown, S., "Interactional Group Therapy with the Adult Children of Alcoholics", *International Journal of Group Psychotherapy, 1982*, 32C37.
2. Rubin, T., *The Angry Book* , Macmillan Publishing Co., New York, 1969.
3. Tiebout, H., "Surrender versus Compliance in Therapy with Special Reference to Alcoholism," The National Council on Alcoholism, Inc., New York, New York, October 3, 1952.


## Separation

1. Peck, M. Scott, *The Road Less Travelled* , Simon and Schuster, New York, 1978.

This book is available at discount
when ordering in quantity.

# ALSO PUBLISHED BY QUOTIDIAN

## *DETACHMENT*

## *ENABLING*

## *THIS NEW DAY*
(A daily meditation book for ACOAs)

## *POTATO CHIPS FOR BREAKFAST*
(Autobiography of a COA)

## FOR THE ABOVE PUBLICATIONS
or
**For an up-to-date catalog
of books on all aspects of
addiction and alcoholism:**

**THOMAS W. PERRIN, INC.
Post Office Box 190
Rutherford, New Jersey 07070**